THE WEAPONS ENCYCLOPÆDIA
TANK AIRCRAFT AFV SHIP ARTILLERY VEHICLES SECRET WEAPON

AF076283

TWE-039 ENG

PANZER I SD.KFZ. 101

THE WEAPONS ENCYCLOPAEDIA

EDITORIAL STAFF

Luca Cristini, Paolo Crippa.

ACADEMIC STAFF

Enrico Acerbi, Massimiliano Afiero, Aldo Antonicelli, Ruggero Calò, Luigi Carretta, Flavio Chistè, Anna Cristini, Carlo Cucut, Salvo Fagone, Enrico Finazzer, Arturo Giusti, Björn Huber, Andrea Lombardi, Aymeric Lopez, Marco Lucchetti, Gabriele Malavoglia, Luigi Manes, Giovanni Maressi, Francesco Mattesini, Daniele Notaro, Péter Mujzer, Federico Peirani, Alberto Peruffo, Maurizio Raggi, Andrea Alberto Tallillo, Antonio Tallillo, Roberto Vela, Massimo Zorza.

PUBLISHED BY

Luca Cristini Editore (Soldiershop), via Orio, 35/4 - 24050 Zanica (BG) ITALY.

DISTRIBUTION BY

Soldiershop - www.soldiershop.com, Amazon, Ingram Spark, Berliner Zinnfigurem (D), LaFeltrinelli, Mondadori, Libera Editorial (Spain), Google book (eBook), Kobo, (eBoook), Apple Book (eBook).

PUBLISHING'S NOTES

None of unpublished images or text of our book may be reproduced in any format without the expressed written permission of Luca Cristini Editore (already Soldiershop.com) when not indicate as marked with license creative commons 3.0 or 4.0. Luca Cristini Editore has made every reasonable effort to locate, contact and acknowledge rights holders and to correctly apply terms and conditions to Content. Every effort has been made to trace the copyright of all the photographs. If there are unintentional omissions, please contact the publisher in writing at: info@soldiershop.com, who will correct all subsequent editions.

LICENSES COMMONS

This book may utilize part of material marked with license creative commons 3.0 or 4.0 (CC BY 4.0), (CC BY-ND 4.0), (CC BY-SA 4.0) or (CC0 1.0). We give appropriate attribution credit and indicate if change were made in the acknowledgments field. Our WTW books series utilize only fonts licensed under the SIL Open Font License or other free use license.

CONTRIBUTORS OF THIS VOLUME & ACKNOWLEDGEMENTS

We would like to thank the main contributors to this issue: The tank profiles are all by the author. The colouring of the photos is by Anna Cristini. Special thanks to national and/or private institutions such as: Army General Staff, State Archives, Bundesarchiv, Nara, Library of Congress, Wikipedia, USAF, Signal magazine, War Chronicles, War Front, IWM, Australian War Museum, etc. A P.Crippa, A.Lopez, Péter Mujzer, L.Manes, C.Cucut, Tallillo archives. Model Victoria (www.modelvictoria.it) etc. for making available pictures or anything else from their archives. Special thanks to all modellers, their clubs and modelling companies for the courtesy use of their images. As far as possible we will always include the names of the authors. Please let us know in case you have not been able to locate them.

For a complete list of Soldiershop titles, or for every information please contact us on our website: www.soldiershop.com or www.cristinieditore.com. E-mail: info@soldiershop.com. Keep up to date on Facebook https://www.facebook.com/soldiershop.publishing

Title: **PANZER I SD.KFZ 101** Code.: **TWE-039 EN**
Series by L. S. Cristini
ISBN code: 979-12-5589-2441 First edition June 2025
THE WEAPONS ENCYCLOPAEDIA (SOLDIERSHOP) is a trademark of Luca Cristini Editore

THE WEAPONS ENCYCLOPÆDIA
TANK AIRCRAFT AFV SHIP ARTILLERY VEHICLES SECRET WEAPON

PANZER I SD.KFZ. 101

LUCA STEFANO CRISTINI

BOOK SERIES FOR MODELLERS & COLLECTORS

CONTENTS

Introduction .... Pag. 5
- Historical context .... Pag. 5
- Development .... Pag. 5
- Vehicle versions .... Pag. 6

Caratteristiche tecniche .... Pag. 21

Versions of the vehicle .... Pag. 27
- The Panzer I becomes a tank destroyer (Panzerjäger) .... Pag. 28
- Sturmpanzer I .... Pag. 28
- Command vehicle (Kleiner Panzerbefehlswagen) .... Pag. 33
- Field experiments and modifications - other vehicles .... Pag. 36

Operational use .... Pag. 41
- Panzer I in the Spanish Civil War .... Pag. 41
- Cooperation with China .... Pag. 45
- Poland, Western Front and WW2 .... Pag. 47

Camouflage and markings .... Pag. 55

Data sheet .... Pag. 57

Bibliography .... Pag. 70

▲ Panzerkampfwagen I Ausf. A (Sd.Kfz. 101) on display at the Deutsches Panzermuseum Munster, Germany. Wiki CC

INTRODUCTION

The **Panzerkampfwagen I**, commonly known as the **Panzer I**, was Germany's first mass-produced tank in the interwar period. Originally designed as a training vehicle, it soon became one of the key tools in the revival of the German armoured force and formed the basis of the Wehrmacht's arsenal in the early stages of the Second World War. The two main versions produced that we will analyse in this volume, **Ausführung A** and **Ausführung B**, share similar characteristics, but also have significant differences, the result of operational experience and the limitations found in the first models.

■ HISTORICAL CONTEXT

The 1919 Treaty of Versailles imposed strict restrictions on defeated Germany, explicitly forbidding the development and production of modern armaments, including tanks. Nevertheless, starting in the 1920s, *Reichswehr* officers began to secretly develop concepts and doctrines for a future armoured force. Clandestine collaborations with the Soviet Union allowed for the training of crews and the development of prototypes in remote territories, such as at the Kama School near Kazan.

It was during this period that the first German experiments with armoured vehicles, such as the **Großtraktor** and **Leichttraktor**, were born, which, although they did not make it past the prototype stage, offered fundamental technical experience. Furthermore, German industries such as **Krupp**, **Rheinmetall** and **Daimler-Benz** were involved early on, hiding their activities under civil names to evade international surveillance.

■ CONCEPTION AND DEVELOPMENT

The development of the Panzer I was influenced by key figures such as General **Oswald Lutz** and especially his chief of staff, Colonel **Heinz Guderian**, who is considered the father of German armoured warfare. Guderian, also inspired by foreign theorists such as the British Percy Hobart, promoted the creation of an autonomous and self-sufficient armoured force. According to his vision, the German army should

▲ Production workshops of the Panzer I, described as an "agricultural tractor" to overcome the limitations of Versailles.

have slow tanks to support the infantry, medium tanks to break the front and heavy tanks to destroy enemy fortifications.

However, while awaiting the development of more sophisticated vehicles such as the **Panzer III** and **Panzer IV**, it was decided to make a light and simple tank that would serve to train crews and test the necessary logistical and industrial chains. Thus was born the **Panzer I**, initially called the **La.S. (Landwirtschaftlicher Schlepper)**, or 'agricultural tractor', to disguise its real military purpose.

Unlike in other countries, Germany distributed production of the Panzer I among several manufacturers. **Krupp** was in charge of the hull, while **Daimler-Benz** was responsible for the superstructure and turrets. Other partners were **Henschel**, **MAN, Grusonwerk** and **Rheinmetall**. This approach made it possible to form an efficient industrial network capable of handling more complex productions in the future.

Production of the Ausf. A was divided into four series (1st-4th Series/La.S.), while the Ausf. B was produced in two main series (5th and 6th Series/La.S.). In total, **1,569 combat tanks** were built, plus several variants for training and command.

■ VEHICLE VERSIONS

From prototype to production: Ausf. A

The first vehicle prefiguring the Panzer I was the **Kleintraktor** designed by Krupp, which adopted a technical layout inspired by the **British Carden-Loyd tankettes**. This vehicle featured a front-engine and rear-wheel drive configuration, later modified in favour of a more efficient rear-engine and rolling train system inspired by the British **Light Tractor**.

The prototype successfully passed the tests in Kummersdorf in 1932, and the go-ahead was given for

▲ The German Panzer I light tank formed the backbone of the German armoured forces for some time. Quickly then the Germans, before anyone else, realised that the winning tank was something else entirely...

▲ One of the very first German military interventions after the First World War was the re-annexation of the Rhur area. On that occasion, it was the Panzer Is that represented the new German army.

PANZER I AUSF. A, 1936

▲ One of the first production examples of the Panzer I Ausf.A (1936) with the original tri-tonal camouflage. This model was among the first light tanks used by the Wehrmacht, initially used for training and in early military operations such as the Spanish Civil War.

the production of the first experimental series. The first 150 examples were without turrets and used for training purposes. Subsequently, the **Ausführung A** version was produced, equipped with a turret armed with **two 7.92 mm MG 13 machine guns**, 13 mm maximum armour and a **60 hp** air-cooled Krupp engine.

This version soon proved to be limited: the armament was ineffective against armoured targets and the propulsion insufficient. Despite this, some **1,190 examples** were produced between 1934 and 1936 in three main series. The Panzer I Ausf. A saw its baptism of fire in the **Spanish Civil War**, when it was supplied by Germany to the Volunteer Troops Corps. There it proved its vulnerability against Soviet T-26 tanks, but also its tactical utility against infantry and light targets.

The evolution: Panzer I Ausf. B

The shortcomings of the A version quickly led to the development of the **Ausf. B**, which introduced significant improvements. The main change was the adoption of a new six-cylinder, water-cooled **Maybach NL 38 TR** engine with power increased to 100 hp. This involved lengthening the hull by about 40 cm, adding an axle with additional load-bearing wheels and a revision of the suspension system, making the vehicle more stable and reliable.

The transmission was also improved, with a new, more robust gearbox. However, the armament and protection remained unchanged, maintaining the limitations already highlighted in the previous version. Between 1936 and 1937, some **399** Ausf. B, plus training and command variants. The Panzer I Ausf. B was used in the same campaigns as the A version, but was quickly overtaken by more powerful vehicles such as the Panzer III and Panzer IV.

▲ The six-cylinder, water-cooled Maybach NL 38 TR engine mounted on the Panzer I.

PANZER I AUSF. A, CHINA, 1937

▲ Panzer I Ausf.A light tank in service with the Kuomintang forces during the Battle of Nanjing. Sent from Germany in tri-tonal camouflage, the vehicle shows faded paintwork, typical of operational wear and tear in Chinese climatic conditions.

PANZER I AUSF. A, GERMANY, 1937

▲ Another variant of the Panzer I Ausf.A (1937) Fahrschule (driving school) version indicated by the chessboard on the turret. This model was among the first light tanks used by the Wehrmacht, initially used for training and in early military operations.

The latest evolutions of the Panzer I: between innovation and obsolescence

As the war progressed, the Panzer I - that little tank born almost by accident - attempted to adapt to the new wartime scenarios. Between 1939 and 1942, two versions radically different from the original models saw the light of day, as if to deny the humble origins of the design. But by then the time for light tanks was coming to an end, and none of these evolutions managed to make a significant mark on the conflict.

The Ausf. C: a scout with teeth

In 1939, when by then the standard Panzer I was considered a relic of the past, Krauss-Maffei and Daimler-Benz set to work transforming it into something completely new. Thus was born the Ausf. C, which retained only the name of the old Panzer I.

It was a vehicle designed for reconnaissance, but with a revolutionary idea: instead of hiding, it could defend itself. The armouring doubled to 30 mm made it tougher, while the armament was a real surprise: a Mauser EW 141 anti-tank rifle, capable of firing armour-piercing bullets that would have made the tank drivers of the first models smile.

The Wehrmacht ordered 46 of them, enough to equip a few select units but too few to make a difference. Two ended up in the 1st Armoured Division in 1943, while the other 38 were sent to Normandy as a mobile reserve, almost an irony of fate for a tank that was created to circumvent the Treaty of Versailles and ended up trying to stop the Allied landings. Some 40 examples were made of this vehicle.

The Ausf. F: a bunker on tracks

If the Ausf. C was an evolution, the Ausf. F was a true rebirth. With its 80 mm of armour on vital parts, this 21-tonne monster was closer to a heavy tank than to a light Panzer I. It was made in about 30 examples, mainly for guerrilla warfare in Yugoslavia.

▲ The Panzer I Ausf. C and also the later Ausf. F were two experiments that came late in the war. Although they borrowed several things from their A and B progenitors, they were completely different tanks with concepts, especially in the armament, that were already outdated.

KLEINER PANZERBEFEHLSWAGEN I AUSF. B, SPAIN, 1937

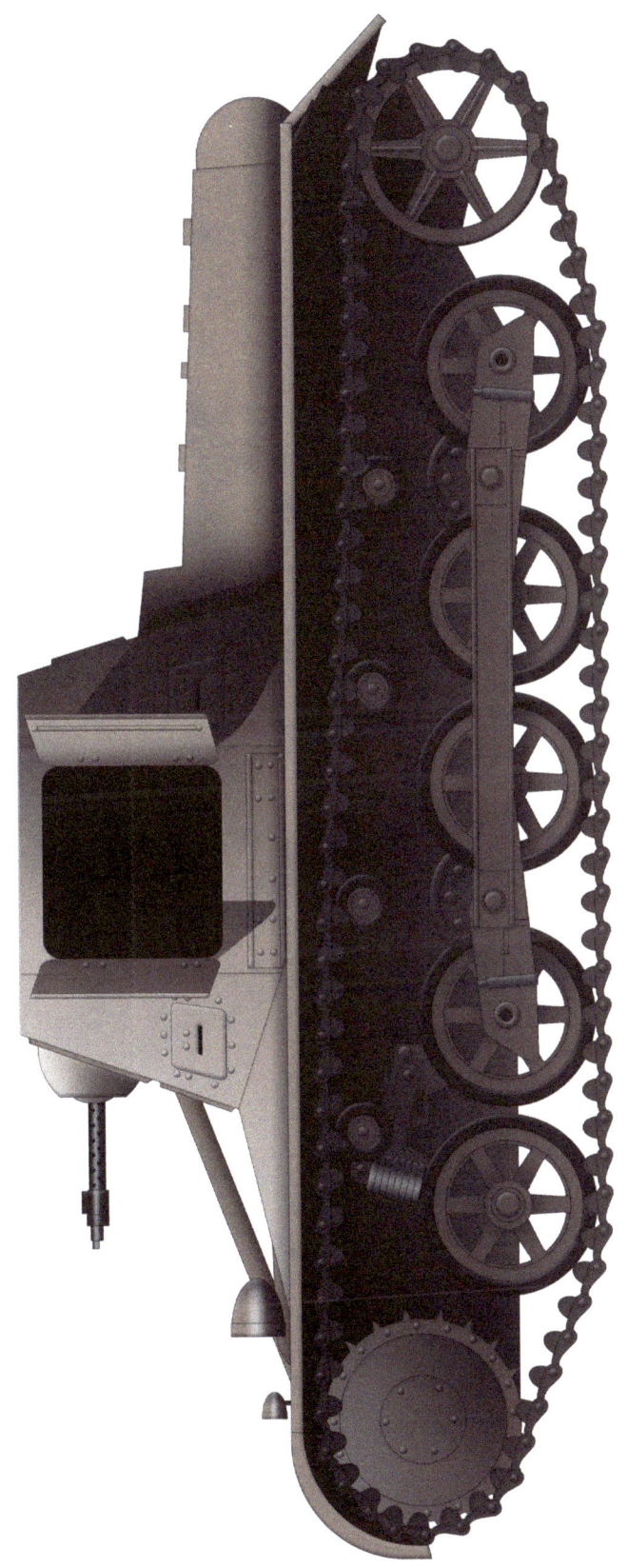

▲ Command version of the Panzer I, employed by the Batallón de Carros de Combate of the Ejército Nacional during the Spanish Civil War. Derived from the Ausf. B, it is distinguished by its raised, unarmoured superstructure, used to coordinate armoured units in the field.

The designers had done away with previous technical solutions: away with the complicated overlapping wheels, replaced by a more conventional five-wheel-per-side system. The new 150-horsepower Maybach engine tried to compensate for the doubled weight, although the top speed of 25 km/h suggested that this was no bolide.

Of the 130 planned, only 30 were built. Eight of these ended up in Kursk in 1943, where their thick armour made them useful in an infantry support role. The others became training vehicles, almost symbolising the fate of an entire generation of tanks: born to fight, finished to teach.

Transformations of the Panzer I: from tank to multi-role platform

Between 1934 and the mid-1940s, the Panzer I lived a second life through numerous variants, born of the need to exploit an outdated frontline vehicle. Already obsolete at its debut due to inadequate armament and too light armour, the small German tank found new life as a versatile platform for specialised roles.

From front line to secondary roles

With the advent of more modern tanks such as the Panzer III and IV, the Panzer I was gradually relegated to auxiliary duties. Its simple and inexpensive hull, however, proved invaluable for development:

- **The Panzerbefehlswagen**: the command version, produced in 200 units on the basis of the Ausf. A and B, equipped with advanced radio equipment to coordinate armoured operations
- **The Panzerjäger I**: the Wehrmacht's first tracked tank destroyer, which mounted an effective 47 mm Czech anti-tank gun. Both of these vehicles are discussed later in the book.

This conversion was not a choice, but a necessity. While German tank fighters faced the Soviet T-34s and American Shermans, the old Panzer I proved that even an outdated design could still serve, albeit in a

▲ An example of Panzer I Ausf. F, formerly at Kursk and preserved at the Patriot Museum in Kubinka, Russia.

PANZER I AUSF. A, POLAND, 1939

▲ Panzer I Ausf. A in action in Poland, 1939. Despite its light armament and thin armour, it was employed en masse for quick breakthroughs, exploiting its mobility. Dull "Panzer grey" camouflage was the initial standard, with little adaptation to the terrain.

different role from its original one. Its most lasting legacy was not as a combat tank, but as an experimental platform that helped German designers develop concepts later applied to more advanced vehicles.

A bitter epilogue

These last versions of the Panzer I tell a story of desperate attempts to keep up with a technological evolution that was now running too fast. They were interesting projects, sometimes even visionary, but arrived too late in a conflict that had already decreed the end of the light tank era.

Perhaps the real lesson of these machines lies in their very existence: they show how even the most humble designs can inspire radical innovations, even if success is not always guaranteed. While their rusty remains ended up in museums or static defence lines, the Panzerwaffe had already turned the page, leaving behind that little tank which, in spite of everything, had helped write the first glorious page of German armoured warfare.

Final considerations

The Panzer I was a vehicle limited in warfare capabilities, but absolutely central to the development of German armoured power. It represented the first concrete step in the creation of the **Blitzkrieg**, providing a technical and tactical test bed for future generations of German tanks. The experiences gained with this small tank were crucial to the development of the more advanced Panzer III, IV and later Panther and Tiger.

Its importance, therefore, should not be sought in its achievements on the battlefield, but in the formative and industrial role it played between 1934 and 1941, marking a turning point in the military history of the 20th century.

▲ The Panzer I Ausf. B looked very similar to the Ausf. A, only it had a reinforced chassis and a more powerful engine. The armament remained unchanged, however.

PANZER I AUSF. B, POLAND, 1939

▲ Light tank Panzerkampfwagen I Ausf. B belonging to the German 4th Panzer Division, moving through the streets of Warsaw during the Polish campaign, September 1939. Equipped with two MG 13 machine guns, it was mainly used for reconnaissance and infantry support.

KLEINER PANZERBEFEHLSWAGEN (SD.KFZ. 265) AUSF. B, 1940

▲ Kleiner Panzerbefehlswagen (Sd.Kfz. 265), light command tank based on the hull of the Panzer I Ausf. B, 1940. Devoid of main armament, it was equipped with enhanced radio equipment for the coordination of armoured units in the field.

▲ Column of Panzer I Ausf. A in training trials in the German countryside; the tanks are accompanied by service trucks.

PANZERJÄGER I AUSF. B, 1940/1941

▲ Panzerjäger I (Sd.Kfz. 101), the first German tank fighter on a Panzer I Ausf. B, armed with a Czech Škoda 4.7 cm PaK(t) gun. Deployed between 1940 and 1941 in France, the Balkans, North Africa and at the beginning of the Russian campaign to face better-armoured enemy tanks.

TECHNICAL FEATURES

In February 1934, after the failure of the first series of La.S., (the abbreviation 'La.S.' refers to the first German light tanks, based on the Carden-Lloyd chassis. These vehicles were initially called '*Landwirtschaftlicher Schlepper*' (agricultural tractor), which was later shortened to 'La.S.') production of the second series of the Panzer I began. While maintaining a similar structure to the previous version, most of the components were redesigned. Among the most significant changes were the enlargement of the return rollers, an increase in fuel tank capacity and the hull height, which was increased by 50 mm. In addition, a radio system was introduced for the first time to improve communication between vehicles, which required the installation of a more powerful electric generator. Before final production, a new cooling system was also implemented, with air filters and air intakes to optimise engine cooling.

■ HULL AND SUPERSTRUCTURE

The hull formed the load-bearing base for the drive system and was composed of welded steel plates. It was separated into two compartments, one for the crew and one for the engine, with a bulkhead dividing them. To reinforce the upper part of the hull, three steel bars were added. Access to the engine and transmission system was via removable hatches. The superstructure, designed by Daimler-Benz, housed a two-man crew and was equipped with a radio system and gas masks, as it had no protection against poisonous gases. The superstructure was divided into two sections: the front section, which protected the crew, and the rear section, which protected the engine and could be easily removed for ease of maintenance. Despite its simplicity, the Panzer I was the first German tank in serial production to include vision slits and bulletproof glass, which resulted in a marked improvement to ensure the safety of the crew.

As for the Ausf. B, the front part of the hull retained the same front configuration as the Ausf. A, while the rear was lengthened to accommodate the new engine and suspension. This lengthening also allowed for better ventilation and the relocation of the tow hook. Openings for draining oil, coolant and fuel were also added, facilitating vehicle maintenance.

The rear armoured lid was redesigned to fit the new engine. It featured a raised section for air intake, necessary for cooling the engine, which was expelled through a grille located on the rear right side of the engine compartment. A new split hatch was added above the engine to facilitate access, while a smaller rectangular hatch was installed above the radiator fan. The two exhaust pipes of the Ausf. A, located on the mudguards, were replaced by a single silencer with armoured protection, mounted at the rear.

At the front, the pilot's periscope was modified, and three bolts with conical heads were added to improve the support of the glass.

Starting with the **5th Series/La.S.**, a reinforcement tube was inserted between the rear deflection wheels to increase structural strength. In addition, a **Nebelkerzenabwurfvorrichtung (N.K.A.V.)** smoke grenade launcher, with five grenades, was introduced after entry into service. Some vehicles also received additional reinforcement for the tube, which tended to break under operational conditions. Finally, starting with the **5b./6th Series**, a new 5.5-litre radiator was installed to replace the previous 3.5-litre one, along with an upgraded cooling fan.

■ TURRETS

The Panzer I turret, derived from the *Kleintraktor* design, was one of the first in production to be mounted on ball bearings, allowing full rotation. Armed with two MG 13 machine guns, it was equipped with slits for vision and a commander's hatch at the top. Despite being visually similar to the *Krupptraktor* turret, the Panzer I version needed only minor modifications on the inside.

The turret of the Ausf. B remained substantially unchanged from the Ausf. A. The commander retained four periscopes and the two machine guns. However, the three lifting hooks were moved from the sides to the top of the turret, thus improving side protection by reducing the exposed bolts.

■ SUSPENSION AND TRANSMISSIONS

The suspension system consisted of a front drive wheel, three return rollers and running wheels, with a spring configuration for the second and third wheels. This system proved problematic, as the idle wheel touched the ground and adversely affected the manoeuvrability of the tank. The transmission had five gears with synchronisation for the first four, but the friction steering system caused difficulties in precision movements.

The most obvious change in the Ausf. B compared to the Ausf. A was the upgrade of the suspension, a distinctive element between the two versions. The modification was aimed at improving the overall mobility and, above all, the manoeuvrability of the vehicle. In the Ausf. A, the movement of the tensioning wheels during steering compromised driving and increased the risk of track loss.

The Ausf. B introduced a fifth load-bearing wheel and a fourth tensioning wheel. The connection between the fourth carrying wheel and the tensioning wheel was removed; the fourth was connected in pairs to the fifth, while the second and third formed another pair. The first wheel remained independent. The tensioning wheel was raised and mounted on an articulated arm housed in a support; track tension was adjusted by rotating the arm.

The propeller shaft transferred torque from the engine through the main clutch. As in the Ausf. A, clutch, transmission and steering unit were connected via flanges to form a single unit.

▲ A Panzer I Ausf. A in the maintenance workshop. The photo allows a good view of some details, such as the engine doors at the rear of the vehicle.

ENGINE

The Panzer I Ausf.A was equipped with a four-cylinder Krupp M305 air-cooled engine, which, although powerful enough (60 horsepower at 2,500 rpm), was extremely noisy, so much so that some soldiers reported that starting the engine could wake up the entire platoon. This problem was so obvious that the tank's manual forbade starting the engine by pushing it. Despite this defect, the engine allowed the Panzer I to reach a maximum speed of 37 km/h.
On the Ausf. B was instead fitted with the water-cooled Maybach NL 38 TR engine, which developed **100 hp at 3,000 rpm**: a significant improvement over the previous air-cooled Krupp M305. This allowed the tank to reach a top speed of around **40 km/h**, which also improved its ability to tackle steep slopes. In addition, the water-cooling system reduced the risk of overheating in hot climates such as Spain or North Africa.
The 6-cylinder engine was cooled by circulating water via a pulley and belt-driven centrifugal pump, which also drove the electric generator. To ensure effective cooling even on inclined slopes, the upper water box directed the liquid to ducts connected to the exhausts. An overhead cam controlled the valves, oil pump, rev counter and magnet. An additional fan was installed next to the engine to facilitate ventilation. The fuel was distributed in two tanks, one **82 litres** and the other **62 litres**, both located on the right side, separated from the crew compartment.

ARMOUR

The armour of the Panzer I consisted of homogenously hardened plates, which provided minimal protection against anti-tank gunfire, but were sufficient to stop small arms bullets. The front of the turret had 15 mm armour, while the superstructure and sides varied between 8 and 14 mm in thickness. The rear was also protected by armour of a similar thickness.
The armour of the Panzer I Ausf. B remained similar to that of the Ausf. A, with 13 mm steel protection at the rear and on the superstructure, but with the engine cover reduced to 8 mm thick. The front of the turret, where the machine guns were mounted, retained 15 mm armour, sufficient to protect against small arms fire and steel-core bullets (SmK) at short distances. Despite the improvements, the protection remained insufficient against larger calibre rounds.

▲ From this picture one can clearly appreciate the suspension and track structure of the small German tank.

PANZER I (FL) AUSF. A CONVERTED TO ARMOURED AMBULANCE, 1940

▲ Panzerkampfwagen I (Fl) Ausf. A converted to armoured ambulance, 1940. Deprived of armament and internally modified for the transport of wounded, it was used in limited numbers on the Western Front for evacuation operations under enemy fire.

▲ The Maschinengewehr 13 (MG 13) Kurz - German light machine gun used on the Panzer I.

ARMAMENT

The Panzer I Ausf.A mounted two MG 13 machine guns, the operation of which was entrusted to the commander. The machine guns were connected to the triggers by cables and could be aimed with either the elevation or rotation knob. Each machine gun could be disconnected to improve firing accuracy. The tank had 2,250 rounds of SmK ammunition in 25 magazines, with a further 61 spare magazines.

As with its predecessor, the Panzer I Ausf. B mounted **two MG 13 Kurz machine guns**, although examples with standard MG 13s were also documented. The commander was responsible for their use. The right machine gun, which was more easily dismounted, was used for direct fire, while the left was more suitable for static covering fire. The MG 13 was the standard weapon of the Reichswehr and Wehrmacht in the early 1930s. Although the MG 34 was available, it was not used on these tanks due to its high cost and tendency to overheat.

▲ Beautiful picture, which better than any other gives the idea of the small size of the Panzer I.

CREW

The crew of the Panzer I (no difference between the Ausf. A and Ausf. B) consisted of only two members, also in view of the cramped space: a driver and a commander/machine gunner. The commander, located in the turret, was responsible for operating the machine guns and radio, as well as giving orders to the driver. Communication between the two was via communication tubes, and many crew members had received adequate training, participating in intensive manoeuvres before the start of the conflict.

▲ A column of Panzer I Ausf. B with the doors wide open, probably due to the heat.

VERSIONS OF THE VEHICLE

HISTORY OF A VERSATILE TANK

The **Panzer I** was born as a temporary solution, a simple training tank designed to teach the new German Panzertruppen the rudiments of armoured warfare. However, its history turned out to be much longer and more complex than expected. By the time war broke out, the Panzer I was already technically outdated, but instead of disappearing from the battlefields, it found new life through a series of conversions and modifications that transformed it into a versatile platform for a variety of roles.

From training to the front: the original versions

The first models, the **Ausf. A** and the **Ausf. B**, were essentially light tanks armed only with machine guns, designed to teach German tankers how to move and fight in formation. The **Ausf. A,** with its modest 57 hp engine, was slow and unprotected, but easy to produce. The **Ausf. B,** with a more powerful engine and an extended chassis, offered slightly better performance, although it remained a very limited vehicle. Despite their shortcomings, these tanks were sent into battle; first during the **Spanish Civil War** and then also in the early stages of the **Second World War**. It soon became clear, however, that the Panzer I was no match for any of the enemy tanks. Rather than withdraw it from service, however, the Germans decided to exploit its versatile chassis to create specialised vehicles.

▲ A Panzerbefehlswagen I Ausf. A photographed in the Soviet Union at the beginning of Operation Barbarossa. BA.

■ PANZER I BECOMES A TANK DESTROYER (PANZERJÄGER)

One of the most famous adaptations was the **Panzerjäger I**, the first German tank fighter on a tracked hull. To make it, the hull of a Panzer I Ausf. B, removed the turret and installed a powerful **47 mm** Czech anti-tank gun on top of it. This vehicle, although improvised, gave German troops a mobile means to counter enemy tanks, at least until the arrival of more advanced models.

The new self-propelled vehicles immediately distinguished themselves in combat during the campaigns in France, North Africa and the USSR (1941). In France, around 100 of these vehicles equipped the 521st, 616th, 643rd and 670th counter-tank battalions. Only the 521st participated from the start, while the other three joined the front line only after training.

In North Africa, Battalion 605 received 27 Panzerjäger I, which arrived in Tripoli between 18-21 March 1941. Despite the reinforcements, the battalion lost 13 vehicles at the beginning of Operation Crusader. Further replacements led to 17 vehicles at the Battle of Al Gazala and 11 at the Second Battle of El Alamein, before the last 2 were sent in November 1942.

■ STURMPANZER I

Another notable conversion was the **15 cm sIG 33 auf Pz.Kpfw.** I, also known as Sturmpanzer I an artillery self-propelled vehicle that mounted a heavy infantry howitzer. The result was an awkward and overloaded vehicle, but one that could provide valuable direct fire support to advancing troops. The Sturmpanzer I, commonly called the Bison, was the first self-propelled artillery vehicle employed by the Wehrmacht during World War II. The vehicle was modified by removing the turret and installing an armoured casemate to house a 150 mm sIG 33 cannon. Produced in limited numbers as an emergency solution, it remained in service exclusively on the Eastern Front until the end of 1943.

▲ 3D drawing of the Sturmpanzer I. Courtesy by Spike78 CC wiki.

INSTANDSETZUNGSKRAFTWAGEN I, FRANCE 1940

▲ Instandsetzungskraftwagen I maintenance vehicle, based on Panzer I and used in 1940 in France. Used by technical units for mechanical repairs in the field, often following armoured columns during the advance.

KLEINER PANZERBEFEHLSWAGEN – FIELD AMBULANCE, FRANCE 1940

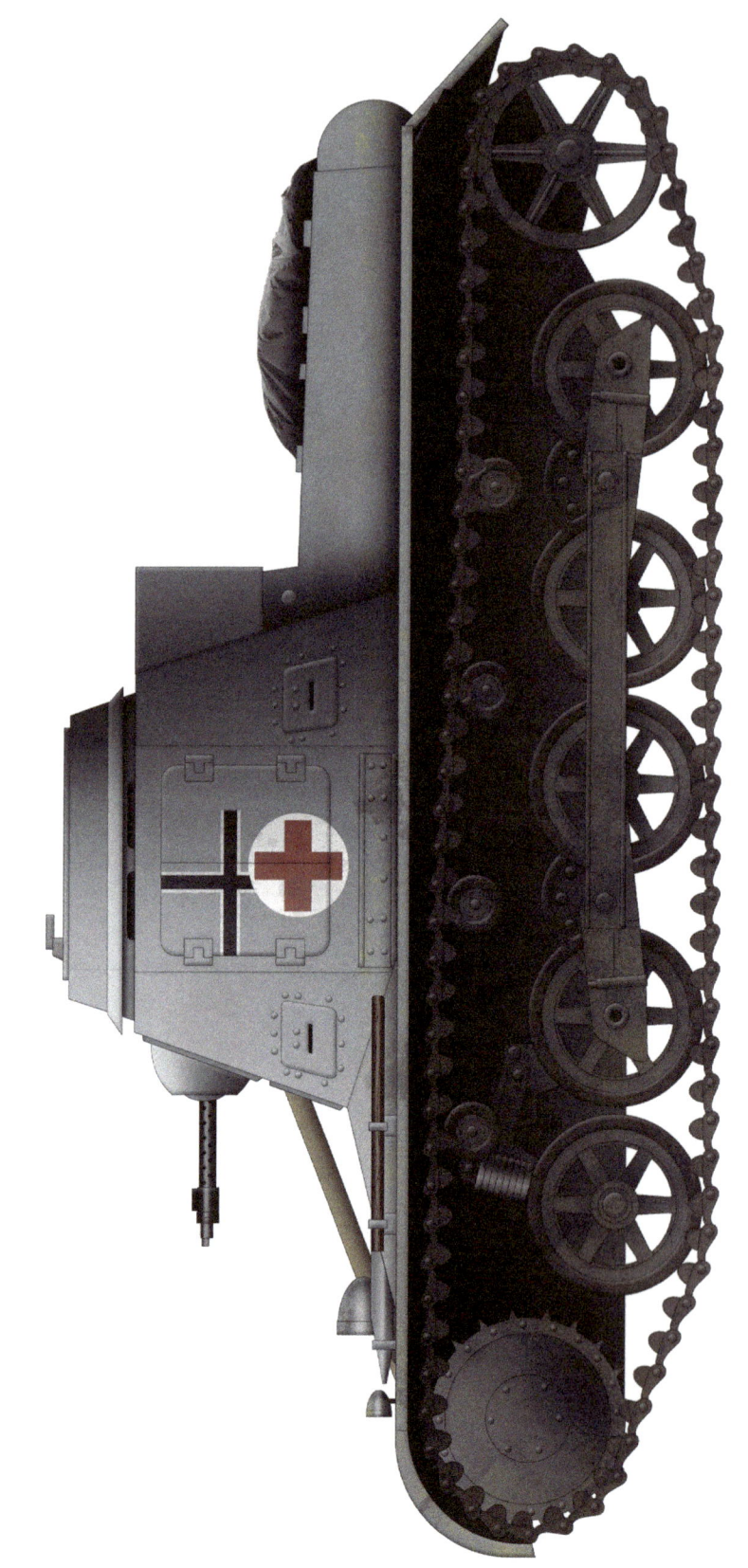

▲ Kleiner Panzerbefehlswagen modified into light armoured ambulance, belonging to the 4th Panzer-Division, in service in France in May 1940. Used to evacuate wounded from the front during the western campaign, with light protection but high mobility.

▲▼▶ A Fahrschulwagen I used as a chassis for the La.S. series (the famous fake tractors).
On the left: a rare picture of two Flakpanzer I 2 cm Flak 38 The anti-aircraft version of the Panzer I. Below: a Sturmgeshutz on the streets of Rostow. Russian campaign 1942. Polish Archive.

PANZER I AUSF. B, HOLLAND 1940

▲ Panzer I Ausf. B of Panzer-Regiment 25, part of Rommel's 7th Panzer-Division, during the campaign in the Netherlands, May 1940. Despite its vulnerability, it was still employed on the front line due to its mobility and ease of deployment.

COMMAND VEHICLES (KLEINER PANZERBEFEHLSWAGEN)

Given the lack of adequate means for the coordination of armoured units, the Panzer I was also converted into a **command vehicle**, the **Kleiner Panzerbefehlswagen Sd.Kfz. 26**. Deprived of its turret, it housed additional radios and a dedicated operator, becoming essential for maintaining communications between departments.

The Sd.Kfz. 265 was developed to meet the German Army's (Heer) need for a command vehicle. The commanders of large armoured units needed to accompany their troops in a vehicle with similar characteristics to those of battle tanks.

In 1935, Krupp presented a design derived from the hull of the training version of the Panzer I Ausf. B, which, being turretless and intended for crew training, proved suitable for conversion into a command vehicle. Between 1935 and 1937, Daimler-Benz produced 190 examples in parallel with the manufacture of the Panzer I Ausf. B.

Operationally, in the years from 1935 to 1940, the Panzerbefehlswagen was the standard command vehicle of the Panzer-Divisions. Each division included 16 armoured companies, organised into 4 battalions, 2 regiments or 1 brigade, with a total of 23 command units, each equipped with at least one such vehicle. From 1940, the Sd.Kfz. 265 was also used in the transmission battalions and observation units of the armoured artillery regiments.

The vehicles also entered combat during the invasion of Poland in September 1939. Later, many of these vehicles were converted into the armoured ambulance *Sanitatskraftwagen I, which was* used in the French campaign in 1940. After the Polish and French campaigns, and starting in 1941, these command tanks crossed the Mediterranean Sea to participate in the North African campaign. They also found extensive use in the Balkan campaign of 1941, before being replaced by larger vehicles.

▲ Disegno in 3D del Kleiner Panzerbefehlswagen Sd.Kfz. 26 Courtesy by Spike78 CC wiki.

▲ 3D drawing of the Munitionsschlepper I ammunition carrier version. Courtesy by Spike78 CC wiki.

PANZER I VARIANTS DATA SHEET		
	Panzerbefehlswagen Sd.Kfz. 26	**Panzerjäger I**
Length	4,45 m	4,14 m
Width	2,08 m	2,01m
Height	1,72 m	2,10 m
Weight	5,8 t	6 t
Crew	3 (commander, attendant and driver)	3 (commander, attendant and driver)
Engine	Maybach NL 38 TR with 100 hp	Maybach NL 38 TR with 100 hp
Maximum speed	37 km/h on road, 12 km/h off road	40 km/h on roada, 15 km/h off road
Developed by	Daimler-Benz	Alkett Industries and later Klöckner-Humboldt-Deutz Industries
Entered service	1938	1940-1941
Armour thickness	6–13 mm	7–13 mm
Armament	A 7.92 mm MG13 machine gun	A 4.7 cm PaK 36 gun (t)
Units	About 190	About 202

▲ Panzer I seen from above.

EXPERIMENTS AND FIELD MODIFICATIONS - OTHER VEHICLES

Other lesser-known conversions included **Munitionsschleppers**, ammunition transport tanks, and even some **Flakpanzers** armed with 20 mm anti-aircraft guns. The latter, although few in number, demonstrated how even an obsolete vehicle could be reused in secondary roles.

Not all variants of the Panzer I were mass-produced. Some remained prototypes, such as the **Brückenleger**, a bridge-carrier that proved too heavy for the hull, or the **Ladungsleger**, designed to place explosive charges against enemy fortifications.

In Spain, the Nazis even experimented with **Panzer I Lanzallamas** equipped with flamethrowers, while their Franco allies modified some examples by fitting them with Italian Breda 20 mm cannons. These attempts, although interesting, were not followed up due to their tactical limitations.

An unsuspected legacy

In the end, the Panzer I survived far beyond expectations. Even when it was withdrawn from the front line, it continued to serve as a **training vehicle**, **artillery tractor** and even as a base for strange experiments, such as remote-controlled demolition tanks.

Its real strength was never its firepower or armour, but its extraordinary adaptability. From the battlefields of Spain to the sands of North Africa, the Panzer I proved that even a seemingly insignificant tank could find its place in military history.

▲ A Panzer I in the Befehlspanzer I command tank version during the invasion of Poland in September 1939 is observed with curiosity by infantry soldiers.

PANZER I AUSF. B, FRANCE 1940

▲ Panzer I Ausf. B of Panzer-Regiment 7, 10th Panzer-Division, France 1940, with two-tone dark grey and earth brown camouflage, typical of the early stages of the conflict. The contrast between the irregular bands was intended to break up the contours of the vehicle in rural French landscapes, but the scheme was soon abandoned in favour of dark grey alone.

▲ Panzer I front and rear.

▲ A Fahrschulwagen I converted into a Funkpanzer (radio vehicle). These Funkpanzers were desperately needed and so the Panzer I chassis proved particularly valuable.

▼ A command vehicle, the Kleiner Panzerbefehlswagen Sd.Kfz. 26, equipped for filming useful for the effective Nazi propaganda apparatus.

PANZER I AUSF. B, HILLAND, MAY 1940

▲ Panzer I Ausf. B of the 9th Panzer-Division near Breda, May 1940. Used in support duties during the invasion of Holland, it has clearly visible markings, a sign of the low need for camouflage due to German air superiority.

OPERATIONAL USE

The Panzer I, despite its limitations, formed the backbone of the German armoured forces until 1941. It was employed **in the Spanish Civil War** (1936-1939), **China, the Polish campaign (1939)**, **the French campaign (1940)**, the **Balkans, North Africa,** and even the first period of the invasion **of the Soviet Union (1941).** In each of these operations, the tank proved useful only against infantry and light positions: its thin armour and lack of anti-tank armament made it easily vulnerable to enemy fire.
With the entry into service of superior vehicles such as the Panzer III and IV, the Panzer I was relegated to secondary tasks: training, command, light reconnaissance. Some hulls were used for self-propelled vehicles or fixed positions along the **Atlantic Wall**.

■ THE PANZER I IN THE SPANISH CIVIL WAR (1936-1939)

The Spanish Civil War represented the Panzer I's baptism of fire. The conflict broke out on 18 July 1936, when Spain plunged into the chaos of civil war, divided between two main factions: the Popular Front (the Republicans) and the Nationalists, led by General Francisco Franco. Soon the conflict took on the characteristics of a proxy war, as foreign powers such as the Soviet Union and Nazi Germany began to send in vehicles, weapons and military advisers to test new tactics and weaponry.
The first foreign contingent to arrive in Spain was Soviet: 50 T-26 tanks arrived on 15 October 1936, representing a significant increase in the Republican offensive capability. The German Kriegsmarine supervised this expedition and Berlin responded immediately: a few days later, 41 Panzer I Ausf. A were sent to Spain, followed by four more batches of Panzer I Ausf. B, totalling about 122. A more detailed report, based on German sources, estimates the arrival in Spain of some 45 Panzer I Ausf.A and 45 Ausf.B, accompanied by four Panzerbefehlswagen I command tanks.

▲ Two Panzer I Ausf. A in Spain, supplied to German volunteer troops during the Civil War 1936-37.

The tanks were entrusted to Lieutenant Colonel Wilhelm Ritter von Thoma, commander of the German armoured contingent known as *Gruppe Thoma* or *Panzergruppe Drohne*, part of the Condor Legion. The first German tanks arrived in Seville on 7 October 1936, while further reinforcements, including 21 Panzer I Ausf.B, arrived on 25 October. Von Thoma set up a training camp near Madrid, in Santa Juana de la Cruz de Cubas de la Sagra, where German advisers, instructors, mechanics and drivers contributed to the creation of two Spanish armoured battalions.

However, the first combat experiences immediately highlighted the shortcomings of the Panzer I. On 30 October 1936, the German tanks clashed with the Soviet BA-6 armoured cars of the *Commune de Paris* battalion, which were equipped with 45 mm cannons that could easily pierce the weak armour of the Panzer I within 500 metres. Shortly before, on 29 October, the first tank battle in the Civil War had occurred near Torrejón de Velasco, where the Republican T-26s had achieved initial success. However, poor coordination with the infantry caused the encirclement and destruction of many Soviet tanks. It was in this encounter that the first documented use of Molotov cocktails against armoured vehicles was also recorded.

The technical superiority of the T-26 was clear. The Panzer I, armed only with 7.92 mm machine guns, was not designed to face other tanks, but rather as an infantry support vehicle. Although at close range (120-150 m) it could damage the T-26s with SMK armour-piercing bullets, the Republicans soon learnt to fight from greater distances, taking advantage of the German tanks' armament inferiority. According to von Thoma, this led to the 'downgrade' of the Panzer I, although this judgement must be put into perspective considering its original purpose.

The need for a more powerful weapon prompted the Nationalist and German leadership to attempt modifications. In 1937, six Panzer I were equipped with the Breda Mod. 1935 20 mm automatic cannon, capable of piercing up to 40 mm of armour at 250 metres. To fit it, it was necessary to radically modify

▲ Panzerkampfwagen I Ausf. A belonging to the Condor Legion, composed of German volunteers sent to fight in the Spanish Civil War alongside nationalist troops.

PANZER I AUSF. A AFRIKA KORPS, JANUARY 1941

▲ One of the first Panzer I Ausf. A landed in North Africa with the Afrika Korps in January 1941. Despite its obsolete armament, it was used for secondary tasks in the early stages of the campaign, adapted to the harsh desert conditions.

▲ A Panzer I Ausf. A that was used during the Spanish Civil War and then remained in Spain as equipment for Francoist troops until the late 1940s. In the background on the left, an Italian light tank can also be seen.

▲ The Chinese in 1937, to counter the Japanese, bought 15 Panzer I, and were also trained by some of the best generals in the German forces. They were later used in the Battle of Nanking.

the turret, opening the upper part and applying an additional vertical structure. The modification proved effective in ballistic terms, but unpopular with German crews, as the open turret was a vulnerable point. Only four examples were completed in Seville; the project was abandoned when Nationalist forces began capturing sufficient numbers of T-26s.

In late 1938, attempts were also made to mount a 45-mm cannon captured from a Soviet T-26 or BT-5 on one Panzer I, and a 37-mm Maklen anti-tank gun supplied by the Soviets to the Asturians on another. However, there is no conclusive evidence that these projects went beyond the experimental phase.

During the conflict, a total of 96 Panzer I Ausf.A, 21 Ausf.B, four Ausf.B command tanks and one unturrettted unit were sent to Spain for training. Despite repeated calls from the Nationalists for tanks equipped with 20 mm cannons, Germany preferred to limit its ground involvement, leaving light panzers to support the infantry. Italy, on the other hand, was much more generous in providing land armament. Combat use also highlighted mechanical problems. The hot Spanish climate caused the engines to overheat, a problem partially solved with the introduction of the Ausf.B version, equipped with a water-cooled engine. The suspension and tracks also suffered from the rough Spanish terrain, while the protection of the embrasures proved insufficient against piercing rifle bullets.

The Panzer Is were often deployed not according to a combined doctrine, but as simple mobile machine-gun nests, advancing in isolation into urban centres. The reduced training of the Spanish crews, compared to the German ones, further reduced their effectiveness. However, on a few occasions the Panzer Is were used more strategically: during the Battle of Brunete in July 1937, von Thoma convinced General Valera to deploy the tanks en masse to break through a weak section of the Republican front. The manoeuvre was initially successful, but the summer heat and fatigue slowed down the advance. A similar tactic was adopted in the great Catalan offensive of December 1938-January 1939, culminating in the fall of Barcelona.

According to the final figures of the war, the Panzer I participated in 904 engagements within the Agrupación de Carros de Combate, becoming a constant presence on almost all fronts of the conflict. Despite its limitations, the Panzer I proved to be more robust and reliable than Soviet tanks in the Spanish environment, thanks in part to the maintenance provided by German and Spanish engineers.

The Republicans also managed to capture some Panzer Is. In at least three documented cases, these vehicles were publicly exhibited in Madrid, without the original machine guns and with armament replaced by light or dummy weapons. One vehicle even displayed a red flag with a hammer and sickle. However, the Republican operational use of German tanks remained limited and sporadic.

In conclusion, the Panzer I - especially the Ausf.B version - played a significant role in the Spanish Civil War, serving as a test bed for the evolution of German armoured warfare. Despite its structural and tactical limitations, it was a key element in the Nationalists' success, paving the way for the innovations that would characterise the Blitzkrieg in World War II.

COOPERATION WITH CHINA

In September 1936, during a period of close cooperation between the Republic of China (ROC) and Nazi Germany, fifteen Panzer I Ausf. A for a total of 1.03 million Reichsmarks. Along with the vehicles, a representative from Krupp, Habermaas, arrived to evaluate their performance. However, upon delivery, the tanks were in very disappointing condition: due to inadequate packaging, numerous components - such as machine gun mounts, brakes and telescopes - were badly oxidised. Some auxiliary materials, such as manuals and toolboxes, were damaged or lost due to contact with salt water, while the moisture in the air had compromised electrical parts, including the cooling fans, causing the engine to overheat by up to 60 °C. The Chinese government falsely accused the Germans of supplying used vehicles, but the condition of the vehicles was actually due to the poor organisation of the Chinese Ordnance Department and the poorly managed transport by the Germans.

This was compounded by serious problems with operational deployment. The suspension of the Panzer I, which had already proved inadequate in Spain, proved even more problematic in China, where the infrastructure was even worse. The only passable areas were dry rice fields, where the vehicle could move with extreme caution. The bumps between the fields were insurmountable, however, and the only other practicable terrain was limited to dry portions near Nanjing. On these muddy soils, the risk of losing a track was always high. In comparison, the Vickers 6-ton and Carden-Loyd tanks exported from Britain proved superior, both in mobility and armament, another weakness of the Panzer I according to Chinese officers.

Ergonomically, the Panzer I was relatively comfortable for the Chinese crews, who were generally shorter in stature than the Germans. However, the vehicle overheated quickly, forcing operators to open visors and hatches, thus exposing themselves to enemy fire. Despite all these limitations, the Panzer I was nevertheless deemed adequate for use by the Chinese National Revolutionary Army (NRA).

In 1937, a dozen Panzer I Ausf. A were used by the 3rd Armoured Battalion of the NRA in the Battle of Nanking against the Imperial Japanese Army. The tanks did not take part in the defence of Shanghai, but fought actively in Nanking, where they were all captured by the Japanese. Some were sent to Japan for analysis and were displayed at the Yasukuni Shrine. For propaganda reasons, and given the consolidation of the alliance between Nazi Germany and the Japanese Empire in an anti-communist key, the Chinese Panzer I were falsely labelled as Soviet-made.

Similar to what happened in Spain, the unsatisfactory performance of the Panzer I in China was due to the fact that the vehicle was not designed for either extreme weather conditions or difficult terrain. Furthermore, as in other contexts, it was not used according to the role for which it was designed, and was quickly overwhelmed by both the environment and the Japanese forces.

▲ German tank Panzer I Ausf. A on the bank of the Brda river in Poland during the German invasion of the country, 4 September 1939. Bundesarchiv. Author's colouring.

POLAND, WEST FRONT AND WW2

In the early stages of the Second World War, German light tanks, such as our *Panzer I*, represented a large part of Germany's armoured force. During the annexation of Austria in March 1938, the German army faced a mechanical failure rate of up to 30 per cent, revealing significant deficiencies in the *Panzerkorps*. This experience prompted Heinz Guderian to upgrade the logistical support to improve its efficiency.

A few months later, in October 1938, Germany occupied the Czechoslovak territory of the Sudetenland and, in March 1939, completed the invasion of Czechoslovakia. This conquest proved to be strategic: Czech tank designs, especially the Panzer 38(t), together with their variants and the production capacity of local factories, were integrated into the *Wehrmacht*. These vehicles, more advanced than the German models of the time, helped strengthen Germany's armoured power, preparing it for the invasion of Poland in September 1939.

Poland (1939)

During the invasion of Poland, the Panzer I represented the backbone of the German armoured divisions: out of approximately 2,700 tanks deployed, more than 970 were Panzer I, to which were added around 260 vehicles in the Ersatzheer reserves. Employed by all the major Panzerdivisions - from the 1st to the 5th, as well as the Kempf Division and the light divisions - the Panzer I made up a substantial share of the vehicle fleet. Despite the lightning success of the campaign, the Panzer I proved to be extremely vulnerable to artillery as well as Polish anti-tank guns, so much so that 89 were reported as total losses at the end of the operation, with the greatest losses suffered by the 4th (46 tanks) and 1st Panzerdivision (25 tanks).

▲ Poland, on the Brda river. Infantrymen on German Panzer I and Panzer II, together with a medium half-track Schützenpanzer (Sd.Kfz. 251/3) with General Heinz Guderian on board, 3 September 1939. Bundesarchiv.

Norway (1940)

In Operation Weserübung, aimed at the occupation of Norway and Denmark, Panzer I were assigned to Panzer-Abteilung z.b.V. 40, which had three companies and three additional armoured platoons. At least 29 Panzer Is operated in Norway, deployed in support of Alpine and mountain troops in the fighting around Narvik and in the western fjords. Eight of them were lost during the operations. Logistical difficulties, the harsh climate and impervious terrain significantly limited the effectiveness of the armoured vehicles.

France and Belgium (1940)

In the course of the French campaign, the Panzer I was once again deployed on a large scale: out of some 2,574 German tanks, as many as 523 were Panzer I, distributed among all Panzerdivisions. Despite its clear technical inferiority compared to French tanks - such as the Somua S-35 or Char B1 - the Panzer I was an integral part of the German success thanks to its doctrinal superiority (Blitzkrieg), better radio communication and inter-force coordination. However, the limitations of the vehicle remained evident: in May 1940 alone, 142 Panzer Is were lost, and another 40 the following June.

Balkans and Greece (1941)

During Operation Marita, the German armoured divisions - particularly the 5th and 9th Panzerdivisions - employed a handful of Panzer Is (9 each). Others were present in the 2nd Panzerdivision, although they were not initially in the assigned strength. Losses were relatively small: three Panzer Is for the 2nd, one for the 5th and three for the 9th Panzerdivision. The mountainous terrain and German numerical superiority in operations made the role of the light tanks marginal.

▲ A Panzer I tank engaged in the campaign to conquer Norway.

North Africa (1941)

Between 8 and 10 May 1941, Panzer-Regiment 5 of the 5. leichte Division landed in Tripoli, inaugurating the German armoured presence in North Africa. At least 25 Panzer Is were deployed, but were quickly withdrawn or abandoned due to their unsuitability for the theatre of operations: the sand, long distances and exposure to Allied artillery made them ineffective and vulnerable. Subsequent *Stärkemeldungen* (force reports) no longer mention them, a sign of their rapid operational exhaustion.

Soviet Union (1941)

Operation Barbarossa, launched on 22 June 1941, marked the last large-scale campaign in which the Panzer I represented a significant component of the German armoured force. Although already considered an antiquated vehicle at the time, this light tank was still present in considerable numbers: out of some 3,300 tanks deployed by the Wehrmacht, as many as 410 were Panzer Is, testifying to the German war industry's shortcomings in promptly replacing older models with modern vehicles. In the first months of the invasion, the Blitzkrieg appeared to repeat the successes achieved in Western Europe: by the end of June, large portions of the Red Army were encircled in the Minsk pocket, and on 21 September, with the fall of Kiev, the Germans were able to turn their forces towards their main strategic objective: Moscow. However, despite their initial successes, between the summer and autumn of 1941 many German commanders realised to their dismay that their tanks were technically inferior to the new Soviet models, in particular the T-34 (medium) and even the heavy KV-1.
The Panzer I, which had already proved to be inadequate during the Spanish Civil War (1936-1939), proved completely incapable of competing with even the lightest armoured vehicles of the Red Army. Even armoured cars like the BA-10, if armed with medium-calibre anti-tank guns, could destroy it with relative ease. On the Northern Front, Army Group North soon realised that none of the German panzer guns could reliably penetrate the frontal armour of the KV-1, leaving the armoured units in serious difficulty against these armoured behemoths.

▲ Greek Front 1941: a Sturmpnazer 15 cm sIG 33 auf Pz.Kpfw. I on a Panzer I type B chassis of the 5th Panzer Division.

KLEINER PANZERBEFEHLSWAGEN I AUSF. B, LIBYA 1941

▲ Kleiner Panzerbefehlswagen I Ausf. B of Panzer-Regiment 5, 21st Panzer-Division, Libya 1941. Retrained as a command tank for the Afrika Korps, it has a sand-yellow camouflage applied locally, more suited to the arid environments of the North African front.

As the Battle of Moscow intensified and the Soviets deployed more and more T-34s and KV-1s, it became clear that the Panzer I no longer had a useful role on the Eastern Front. Some examples, now considered too vulnerable for direct combat, were converted back into logistical support vehicles, used to haul trucks and other light vehicles through the Russian autumn mud, attempting to alleviate the growing difficulties of resupply. Others, however, were relegated to secondary tasks, such as anti-partisan combat or rear protection, used to guard airfields, depots and other military infrastructure in occupied territories. The Russian campaign thus marked the operational end of the Panzer I, a vehicle conceived in the 1930s as a temporary solution and now completely outmoded by the demands of increasingly advanced mechanised warfare.

Its persistence in the ranks of the Wehrmacht until 1941 was more a symptom of German production shortcomings than a strategic choice, and the confrontation with Soviet armoured vehicles decreed its irremediable obsolescence. A total of 415 Panzer Is were declared as total losses in 1941.

▲ The rapid French campaign saw success thanks to the armoured component well manoeuvred by German generals, in which the small Panzer I also took part. Above: a Panzer I Ausf. B in Calais guards some British prisoners of war.

PANZERJÄGER I AUSF. B OF THE 5ᵀᴴ LEICHTE DIVISION, LIBYA 1941

▲ Panzerjäger I (4.7 cm PaK) on Ausf. B of the 5th Leichte Division, Libya 1941. Still in standard European dark grey livery, typical of the first vehicles sent into the desert before the introduction of sand paint by the Afrika Korps.

▲ A command tank radio version Kleiner Panzerbefehlswagen Sd.Kfz. 26.

▼ A Panzer I tank company during the early stages of Operation Barbarossa, busy crossing the endless wheat fields of the Ukraine.

PANZER I SD.KFZ. 101

PANZER I AUSF. A, SIDI OMAR, SEPTEMBER 1941

▲ Panzer I Ausf. A of Panzer-Regiment 5, 21st Panzer-Division, at Sidi Omar, along the Libyan-Egyptian border, September 1941. At this stage the Afrika Korps was engaged in static fighting and armed reconnaissance after the failed assault on Tobruk. The now obsolete tank was used for patrols and light support, often with locally applied sand livery.

CAMOUFLAGE AND MARKINGS

■ CAMOUFLAGE

The first Panzer I Ausf. B were painted with the standard three-tone camouflage used between 1932 and 1937, known as *Buntfarbenanstrich* (German: 'multicoloured scheme'), characterised by yellow, green and brown spots.

In June 1937, an order was issued to paint all newly produced vehicles in dark grey with brown spots. The following year, in 1938, the existing vehicles were also ordered to be repainted according to this new scheme. During the Polish campaign and in the early stages of the invasion of France in 1940, the Panzer I maintained this two-tone camouflage.

After the invasion of France, to save paint, it was decided to remove the brown stains, leaving the vehicles completely in dark grey. The Panzer I Ausf. B sent to North Africa were instead painted in the colours of the Afrika Korps: a yellow base with yellow-green spots. Starting in 1943, all vehicles were ordered to be painted in dark yellow (*Dunkelgelb*), including some of the few Ausf. B still in service.

■ DIVISIONAL INSIGNIA AND IDENTIFICATION SYMBOLS

Before the introduction of national symbols such as the *Balkenkreuz* (beam cross) and numerical identification systems, the first Panzer Is - as well as French and other nations' tanks - used symbols inspired by playing cards. This practice, however, was limited to the first manoeuvres and parades of the newly formed Panzerdivision between 1935 and 1937.

▲ A Panzer I with its Balkenkreuz on display at the United States Army Ordnance Museum (Aberdeen Proving Ground, MD). By Mark Pellegrini, courtesy of Wiki cc.

Later, the Panzer I adopted a system consisting of numbers, colours and shapes, applied with stencils on the driver's front plate and rear plates. This method was used until the Polish campaign, although many units ignored it, preferring the three-digit number system, which eventually became the standard. During exercises, a chequered ring around the turret indicated platoon or company commanders. In the early years, other symbols were also used, the meaning of which is not always clear.

The rear plate, attached to the turret or bonnet, was a light grey rectangle measuring 420 mm by 240 mm, with two symbols in the centre. On the right was a coloured rhombus with a regimental identification number, while on the left two red stripes indicated a platoon commander and a red circle a company commander.

Other symbols included:
- white square = 1st platoon
- two white stripes = 2nd platoon
- triangle = 3rd platoon

The filling colour of the rhombus identified the company:
- white = 1st/5th
- red = 2nd/6th
- yellow = 3rd/7th
- light blue = 4th/8th

A solid rhombus indicated the I. Abteilung (1st battalion), while one with a black stripe represented the II. Abteilung (2nd battalion).

The three-digit number system was located on the sides or front of the superstructure. Before the war it was very complex, but during the conflict it was simplified to such an extent that it became obvious to the enemy which vehicles were platoon commanders - favourite targets for anti-tank guns. This led to its gradual decommissioning and the creation of customised systems by units. In this system:

- the first number indicated the company
- the second the platoon
- the third the individual tank

In the absence of the third number, the tank belonged to the *Leichte Zug* (light platoon) or the *Stab* (command).

The colour of the filling identified the battalion (white = 1st, red = 2nd) and initially a dot was used instead of a zero, which was later replaced.

Shortly before the war, in order to standardise markings, it was ordered that full white *Balkenkreuze* be painted on the sides and turrets of the tanks. Without these, a vehicle could be mistaken for an enemy. A white square for aerial recognition was also painted on the engines, later removed to avoid friendly fire. It was later replaced by the *Fliegertuch* (aerial reconnaissance cloth), often a Nazi flag used mainly on the Eastern Front and in Africa.

However, the white Balkenkreuz attracted enemy fire and many crews covered it with mud or repainted it yellow. To remedy the problem, Balkenkreuze with a blank centre on the sides and back were ordered in October 1939. Between 1940 and 1941, a black centre stripe was added to improve camouflage.

With the start of the war, the tanks were assigned to Panzerdivisionen instead of regiments, and each division received a specific insignia, applied in yellow on all armoured and motorised vehicles. No compulsory location was defined for these insignia, but the high command provided instructions on their appearance. During the conflict, new symbols were introduced or old ones replaced to disguise the identity of the divisions.

▲ Panzer I Ausf. A, stored at the Swedish Tank Museum Arsenalen, Strängnäs, Sweden, in 2013 wiki CC.

DATA SHEET		
	Panzer I Ausf. A	**Panzer I Ausf. B**
Length	4,02 m	4,42 m
Width	2,06 m	2,06 m
Height	1,72 m	1,72 m
Weight	5,4 t	5,8 t
Crew	2 (commander/taker and driver)	2 (commander/taker and driver)
Engine	Krupp M 305 with 57 hp	Maybach NL 38 TR with 100 hp
Maximum speed	37 km/h on road, 12 km/h off road	40 km/h on road, 15 km/h off road
Developed by	Henschel, MAN, Krupp, Daimler-Benz	Henschel, MAN, Krupp, Daimler-Benz
Entered service	1934	1935–1936
Armour thickness	7–13 mm	7–13 mm
Armament	2 × MG13 7.92 mm machine guns	2 × MG34 7.92 mm machine guns
Units	About 818	About 675

PANZER I AUSF. B, EL AGHEILA, MARCH 1941

▲ Panzer I Ausf. B of Panzer-Regiment 5, 5th Leichte Division, at El Agheila, March 1941. Among the first German vehicles to go into action in North Africa, it was employed during the initial advance of the Afrika Korps against the retreating British forces from Cyrenaica.

PANZER I AUSF. B, FRANCE, 1940

▲ Panzer I Ausf.B in action in France 1940. This example belonged to the 31st Panzer Regiment of the 5th Panzer Division.

SELF-PROPELLED ARTILLERY ON THE HULL OF PANZER I AUSF. B, GREECE, APRIL 1941

▲ Heavy artillery self-propelled 15 cm sIG 33 mounted on the hull of Panzer I Ausf. B, employed during the invasion of Greece, April 1941. Used in infantry support in mountain fighting, it was powerful but extremely vulnerable due to its exposed structure and excessive weight on the light frame.

▲ German troops during the invasion of France: an ammunition-carrying Panzer I crosses a makeshift bridge over a stream.

▼ Russia, July 1942: a Sturmpanzer 15 cm sIG 33 auf Pz.Kpfw. I on a Panzer I type B chassis. Bundesarchiv.

FLAKPANZER I ON PANZER HULL I AUSF. A, EASTERN FRONT 1942

▲ Flakpanzer I armed with a 2 cm FlaK 38 gun on the hull of Panzer I Ausf. A, a very rare version designed to provide anti-aircraft cover for mobile units. Modified in 1942, it was used in small numbers on the Eastern Front, where the limited protection and light armament made its use risky but valuable.

▲ Columns of Pz.Kpfw. entered the town of Åbenrå during the occupation of Denmark on 9 April 1940.

▼ Panzer I Ausf. A tanks cross a bridge over the Loire in Tours, France in 1940. The tanks belong to the 7th Panzer Division.

PANZER I MODIFIED FOR DEMOLITION TASKS, EASTERN FRONT 1942

▲ Special version of the Panzer I used as a demolition vehicle, armed with explosive charges or pioneer equipment. Used on the Eastern Front in 1942 for the destruction of fortifications or barrages, it exploited the light hull of the Panzer I for high-risk assault operations.

▲ A Ladungsleger I, an Engineer Corps demolition tank. Eastern Front 1942.

► The Panzer I Ausf.A (1937) Fahrschule (driving school) version indicated by the chessboard on the turret.

▼ A Kleiner Panzerbefehlswagen Sd.Kfz. 26., next to a Panzer I, both unarmed, in an army depot.

PANZER I SD.KFZ. 101

GERMAN TANK FIGHTER ON PANZER I AUSF. B, CAPTURED BY THE SOVIETS, AUGUST 1942

▲ German 4.7 cm PaK(t) fighter on Panzer I Ausf. B, captured and reused by the Soviets, August 1942. Originally employed by the Wehrmacht on the Eastern Front, this rare specimen shows the adaptation of Czech anti-tank weapons on light frames, used in emergencies against T-34s.

▲ Column of Panzer I Ausf. A in pre-war training.
▼ Panzer I tanks parade through the Sudetenland villages newly occupied by Hitler's army.

FIRST TYPE KLEINER PANZERBEFEHLSWAGEN I AUSF. B, POLAND 1939

▲ The first Kleiner Panzerbefehlswagen originally had a relatively simple superstructure without a commander's turret. This example is pictured serving in an unknown unit in Poland in 1939.

▲ Shot of a line of Panzer I Ausf. A at the Panzertruppenschule (Armoured Corps School) in Wunsdorf in 1937.

BIBLIOGRAPHY

- Anderson Thomas, *The History of the Panzerwaffe Volume 1*.
- Barbarito Jacopo, *I panzer di Hitler: I carri armati tedeschi dalle origini alla Seconda Guerra Mondiale* 2023 Soldiershop. Italy (also in English version)
- Baxter I.M. *Achtung Panzer (Armor at War Series)* Concord edition 2002
- Bauer Hans-Jürgen Die deutsche Panzerwaffe im 2. Weltkrieg: Panzer I (German Edition), 2024
- Bishop Chris, *Weapons of World War II* (London: Brown Packaging Books Ltd, 1998).
- Carruthers Bob, *Panzer I & II: Germany's Light Tanks* (Hitler's War Machine Series).
- Daley John, "Soviet and German Advisors Put Doctrine to the Test: Tanks in the Siege of Madrid", in *Armor* (Fort Knox, KY: US Army Armor Center, May 1999).
- David Miller, *Illustrated Directory of Tanks and Fighting Vehicles: From World War I to the Present Day* (St. Paul, MN: Zenith Press, 2000).
- Doyle David e Jeff Kleinhenz, *German Panzer I: A Visual History of the German Army's WWII Early Light Tank* (Visual History Series)
- De Sisto Frank V. , *German Leichte Panzer at War* (Armor at War Series).
- Guderian Heinz, *Panzer Leader* (New York: Da Capo, 1996).
- Hahn Fritz, *Waffen und Geheimwaffen des deutschen Heeres 1933–1945* (Eggolsheim: Dörfler Verlag, 2003).
- Haupt Werner , The History of the Panzer Troops 1916-1945. Schiffer edition 1997.
- Kurowski Franz e David Johnston *Panzer Aces I: Battle Stories of German Tank Commanders in WWII* Stackpole Books 2022
- Jackson Robert , *Panzer I & II: Blueprint for Blitzkrieg 1933–1941* (TankCraft) 2018
- Ledwoch Janusz, *PzKpfw I Vol. I* (Tank Power, Vol. XI). Wydawmictwo Militaria Polonia
- Lucas Molina Franco & José Mª Manrique García, *Blindados Alemanes en el Ejército de Franco (1936–1939)* (Valladolid: Galland Books, 2008).
- Lucas Molina Franco, *Panzer I: The Beginning of a Dynasty*.
- Paul Thomas, *Hitler's Light Tanks 1935–1943* (Images of War).
- Pére Artemio Mortera, , *Los Medios Blindados de la Guerra Civil Española. Teatro de Operaciones del Norte 36/37* (Valladolid: AF Editores, 2007).
- Perrett Bryan, *German Light Panzers 1932–1942* (Osprey Vanguard).
- Peter McCarthy & Mike Syron, *Panzerkrieg: The Rise and Fall of Hitler's Tank Divisions* (New York: Carroll and Graf, 2002).
- Scheibert Horst *Panzer I Paperback* – January 13, 1997, Schiffer edtion
- Scheibert Horst, Uwe Feist, Mike Dario, *Panzer I* (Waffenarsenal).
- Spielberger *Walter Panzers I and II and their Variants: from Reichswehr to Wehrmacht*, 2007
- Spielberger Walter J. , *Die Panzerkampfwagen I und II und ihre Abarten* (Motorbuch Verlag, 1974).
- Thomas L. Jentz & Hilary Louis Doyle, *Panzer Tracts No. 1-1: Panzerkampfwagen I, Kleintraktor to Ausf. B*.
- Thomas L. Jentz & Hilary Louis Doyle, *Panzer Tracts No. 1-2: Panzerkampfwagen I, Kl. Pz. Bef. Wg. to VK 18.01*.
- Tucker-Jones Anthony , *Panzer I and II: The Birth of Hitler's Panzerwaffe* (Images of War) 2018

PUBLISHED TITLES

TWE-039 EN